LIFE'S LITTLE
INSTRUCTION BOOK

Volume II

by H. Jackson Brown, Jr.

Rutledge Hill Press
Nashville, Tennessee

Published in Nashville, Tennessee, by Rutledge Hill Press, Inc..
211 Seventh Avenue North, Nashville, Tennessee 37219. Distributed
in Canada by H. B. Fenn and Company Ltd., Mississauga, Ontario.

Typography by D&T/Bailey Typesetting, Nashville, Tennessee

Library of Congress Cataloging-in-Publication Data

Brown, H. Jackson, 1940–
    Life's little instruction book.

    1. Happiness—Quotations, maxims, etc.   2. Conduct
of life—Quotations, maxims, etc.   I. Title.
    BJ1481.B87   1991   170′.44   91-9800
ISBN 1-55853-102-5 (v. 1, paperback)
ISBN 1-55853-121-1 (v. 1, hardcover)
ISBN 1-55853-216-1 (v. 2)

Printed in the United States of America
1 2 3 4 5 6 7 8 9 10 11 12—94 93

INTRODUCTION

LIFE is a process. We are all works in progress—
green tomatoes ripening on the windowsill of life.
As I experience more, learn more, and contemplate
more, I often think of what use my discoveries
might be to my son, Adam.

Several years ago I jotted down a list of advice for
him as he left home to begin college. At the time I
thought the list was fairly complete. But within a
few days of presenting him with the 32 typed pages
that became *Life's Little Instruction Book,* I began to
think of other entries I wished I had included. How

could I have forgotten to mention "Never be the first to break a family tradition," or "Believe in love at first sight," or practical advice like "Get a flu shot" and "Never drive while holding a cup of coffee between your knees"? Obviously there was only one thing to do—start another list. I promised myself I wouldn't send it to him until it reached at least 512 entries—one more than the original list. It took two years to complete.

The day Adam received it, he called from his apartment. "Dad," he said, "this new list is terrific. I think it's more useful than the first one. Does this mean I should look for a new volume of *Life's Little Instruction Book* every two years?" "Would you like that?" I asked. "Oh, yes," he said. "I'll see what I can do," I replied, with not a small degree of satisfaction.

Little does Adam know that I can no more stop writing down these suggestions and observations than I could stop at a doughnut shop and order only coffee.

Life keeps coming at me, and new insights and discoveries get caught in my net. Like a fisherman, I haul them up, sort the catch, and head for the harbor. It's late and getting dark. But up ahead, standing on the dock, is a young man holding a lantern welcoming me. It's my son, Adam.

Other books by H. Jackson Brown, Jr.

A Father's Book of Wisdom
P.S. I Love You
Life's Little Instruction Book
Live and Learn and Pass It On

512 · Believe in love at first sight.

513 · Never laugh at anyone's dreams.

514 · Overpay good baby sitters.

515 · Never refuse jury duty. It is your civic responsibility, and you'll learn a lot.

516 · Accept a breath mint if someone offers you one.

517 · When you feel terrific, notify your face.

518 · Love deeply and passionately. You might get hurt, but it's the only way to live life completely.

519 · Never apologize for being early for an appointment.

520 · Open the car door for your wife and always help her with her coat.

521 · Discipline with a gentle hand.

522 · When reconvening after a conference break, choose a chair in a different part of the room.

523 · Read the ten books nominated each year for the ABBY Award.

524 · Rake a big pile of leaves every fall and jump in it with someone you love.

525 • Volunteer. Sometimes the jobs no one wants conceal big opportunities.

526 • Never drive while holding a cup of hot coffee between your knees.

527 • Carry Handi-Wipes in your glove compartment.

528 • Use a travel agent. It costs no more and saves time and effort.

529 · Have a professional photo of yourself
made. Update it every three years.

530 · Never miss an opportunity to ride a
roller coaster.

531 · Never miss an opportunity to have
someone rub your back.

532 · Never miss an opportunity to sleep on
a screened-in porch.

533 · Sign all warranty cards and mail them in promptly.

534 · Remember the advice of our friend Ken Beck: When you see a box turtle crossing the road, stop and put it safely on the other side.

535 · Create a little signal only your wife knows so that you can show her you love her across a crowded room.

536 · Never be the first to break a family tradition.

537 · Park next to the end curb in parking lots. Your car doors will have half the chance of getting dented.

538 · Keep a diary of your accomplishments at work. Then when you ask for a raise, you'll have the information you need to back it up.

539 · Never sign contracts with blank spaces.

540 · Drive as you wish your kids would. Never speed or drive recklessly with children in the car.

541 · In disagreements, fight fairly. No name calling.

542 · Never take the last piece of fried chicken.

543 · Ask about a store's return policy when you purchase an item that costs more than $50.

544 · When you go to borrow money, dress as if you have plenty of it.

545 · Never pick up anything off the floor of a cab.

546 · Don't judge people by their relatives.

547 · Eat a piece of chocolate to cure bad breath from onions or garlic.

548 · Seize every opportunity for additional training in your job.

549 · When traveling, leave the good jewelry at home.

550 · Put your address inside your luggage as well as on the outside.

551 · Never give your credit card number over the phone if you didn't place the call.

552 · Remember that everyone you meet is afraid of something, loves something, and has lost something.

553 · Check hotel bills carefully, especially the charges for local and long-distance calls.

554 · Talk slow
but think quick.

555 · When someone asks you a question you don't want to answer, smile and ask, "Why do you want to know?"

556 · Don't admire people for their wealth but for the creative and generous ways they put it to use.

557 · Take along two big safety pins when you travel so that you can pin the drapes shut in your motel room.

558 · Never betray a confidence.

559 · Never claim a victory prematurely.

560 · Never leave the kitchen when something's boiling on the stove.

561 · Say "bless you" when you hear someone sneeze.

562 · Make the punishment fit the crime.

563 · Remember that just the moment you say, "I give up," someone else seeing the same situation is saying, "My, what a great opportunity."

564 · Tour the main branch of the public library on Fifth Avenue the next time you are in New York City. Unforgettable.

565 · Never give anybody a fondue set or anything painted avocado green.

566 ◆ Don't let your family get so busy that you don't sit down to at least one meal a day together.

567 ◆ Remember the three Rs: Respect for self; Respect for others; Responsibility for all your actions.

568 ◆ Carry your own alarm clock when traveling. Hotel wake-up calls are sometimes unreliable.

569 · When you lose, don't lose the lesson.

570 · Keep the porch light on until all the family is in for the night.

571 · Plant zucchini only if you have lots of friends.

572 · Take along a small gift for the host or hostess when you're a dinner guest. A book is a good choice.

573 • Don't overlook life's small joys while searching for the big ones.

574 • Keep a well-stocked first-aid kit in your car and at home.

575 • Never be photographed with a cocktail glass in your hand.

576 • Don't let a little dispute injure a great friendship.

577 • Don't marry a woman who picks at her food.

578 • Order a seed catalog. Read it on the day of the first snowfall.

579 • Pack a compass and the Nature Company's pocket survival tool when hiking in unfamiliar territory.

580 • Read a book about beekeeping.

581 · When lost or in distress, signal in "threes"—three shouts, three gunshots, or three horn blasts.

582 · Don't be surprised to discover that luck favors those who are prepared.

583 · When asked to play the piano, do it without complaining or making excuses.

584 · Subscribe to *Consumer Reports* magazine.

585 · Don't expect your love alone to make a neat person out of a messy one.

586 · Take off the convention badge as soon as you leave the convention hall.

587 · Look for ways to make your boss look good.

588 · Every so often, invite the person in line behind you to go ahead of you.

589 · Carry a small pocket knife.

590 · Remember that the person who steals an egg will steal a chicken.

591 · Meet regularly with someone who holds vastly different views than you.

592 · Don't go looking for trouble.

593 · Don't buy someone else's trouble.

594 · Give people more than they expect and do it cheerfully.

595 · Be the first to fight for a just cause.

596 · When you have the choice of two exciting things, choose the one you haven't tried.

597 · Remember that no time spent with your children is ever wasted.

598 · Remember that no time is ever wasted that makes two people better friends.

599 ◆ Avoid approaching horses and restaurants from the rear.

600 ◆ There are people who will always come up with reasons why you can't do what you want to do. Ignore them.

601 ◆ Check to see if your regular car insurance covers you when you rent a car. The insurance offered by car rental companies is expensive.

602 · If you need to bring in a business partner, make sure your partner brings along some money.

603 · Never say anything uncomplimentary about another person's dog.

604 · If you have trouble with a company's products or services, go to the top. Write the president, then follow up with a phone call.

605 · Don't ride in a car if the driver has been drinking.

606 · Call the Better Business Bureau if you're not sure about a business' reputation.

607 · Think twice before accepting the lowest bid.

608 · Never miss a chance to dance with your wife.

609 · When in doubt about what art to put on a wall, choose a framed black-and-white photo by Ansel Adams.

610 · When uncertain what to wear, a blue blazer, worn with gray wool slacks, a white shirt, and a red-and-blue striped silk tie, is almost always appropriate.

611 · When boarding a bus, say "hello" to the driver. Say "thank you" when you get off.

612 · Write a short note inside the front cover when giving a book as a gift.

613 · Never give a gift that's not beautifully wrapped.

614 · Make the rules for your children clear, fair, and consistent.

615 · Don't think expensive equipment will make up for lack of talent or practice.

616 • Learn to say "I love you" in French, Italian, and Swedish.

617 • On a clear night, look for Orion's Belt and think of your mother. It's her favorite constellation.

618 • Memorize your favorite love poem.

619 • Ask anyone giving you directions to repeat them at least twice.

620 · When you are totally exhausted but have to keep going, wash your face and hands and put on clean socks and a clean shirt. You will feel remarkably refreshed.

621 · Make allowances for your friends' imperfections as readily as you do for your own.

622 · Steer clear of any place with a "Ladies Welcome" sign in the window.

623 · When you realize you've made a mistake, take immediate steps to correct it.

624 · Be ruthlessly realistic when it comes to your finances.

625 · Smile when picking up the phone. The caller will hear it in your voice.

626 · Set high goals for your employees and help them attain them.

627 · Pay your bills on time. If you can't, write your creditors a letter describing your situation. Send them something every month, even if it's only five dollars.

628 · Do your homework and know your facts, but remember it's passion that persuades.

629 · Don't waste time trying to appreciate music you dislike. Spend the time with music you love.

630 · Always put something
in the collection plate.

631 · When concluding a business deal and
the other person suggests working out the
details later, say, "I understand, but I
would like to settle the entire matter
right now." Don't move from the table
until you do.

632 · Ask yourself if you would feel comfortable
giving your two best friends a key to
your house. If not, look for some new best
friends.

633 · Do the right thing, regardless of what others think.

634 · Wear a shirt and tie to job interviews, even for a job unloading boxcars.

635 · Judge people from where they stand, not from where you stand.

636 · When shaking a woman's hand, squeeze it no harder than she squeezes yours.

637 · Be open and accessible. The next person you meet could become your best friend.

638 · Never wash a car, mow a yard, or select a Christmas tree after dark.

639 · Life will sometimes hand you a magical moment. Savor it.

640 · Learn how to make tapioca pudding and peanut brittle in the microwave.

641 · Set aside your dreams for your children and help them attain their own dreams.

642 · Dress a little better than your clients but not as well as your boss.

643 · Take the stairs when it's four flights or less.

644 · Never threaten if you don't intend to back it up.

645 • Learn to save on even the most modest salary. If you do, you're almost assured of financial success.

646 • Buy a used car with the same caution a naked man uses to climb a barbed-wire fence.

647 • Hold yourself to the highest standards.

648 • Buy the big bottle of Tabasco.

649 · Don't confuse comfort with happiness.

650 · Don't confuse wealth with success.

651 · Be the first to forgive.

652 · When talking to your doctor, don't let him or her interrupt or end the session early. It's your body and your money. Stay until all your questions are answered to your satisfaction.

653 · Whenever you take something back for an exchange or refund, wear a coat and tie.

654 · Check for toilet paper *before* sitting down.

655 · If you work for an organization that makes its decisions by committee, make darn sure you're on the committee.

656 · Don't stop the parade to pick up a dime.

657 · Make a habit of reading something inspiring and cheerful just before going to sleep.

658 · Marry a woman you love to talk to. As you get older, her conversational skills will be as important as any other.

659 · Turn enemies into friends by doing something nice for them.

660 · When hiring, give special consideration to anyone who's been an Eagle Scout.

661 · Be as friendly to the janitor as you are to the chairman of the board.

662 · Never buy anything electrical at a flea market.

663 · Remember that a person who is foolish with money is foolish in other ways too.

664 • If you want to do something and you feel in your bones that it's the right thing to do, do it. Intuition is often as important as the facts.

665 • Don't cut corners.

666 • Learn to bake bread.

667 • Everyone loves praise. Look hard for ways to give it to them.

668 · Spend some time alone.

669 · Be an original. If that means being a little eccentric, so be it.

670 · Everybody deserves a birthday cake. Never celebrate a birthday without one.

671 · Pay as much attention to the things that are working positively in your life as you do to those that are giving you trouble.

672 ◆ Open your arms to change, but don't let go of your values.

673 ◆ When it comes to worrying or painting a picture, know when to stop.

674 ◆ Don't expect anyone to know what you want for Christmas if you don't tell them.

675 ◆ Before taking a long trip, fill your tank and empty your bladder.

676 • Ask for double prints when you have film processed. Send the extras to the people in the photos.

677 • When taking a woman home, make sure she's safely inside her house before you leave.

678 • Live with your new pet several days before you name it. The right name will come to you.

679 · Every year celebrate the day you and your wife had your first date.

680 · Treat your employees with the same respect you give your clients.

681 · Slow down. I mean *really* slow down in school zones.

682 · Allow your children to face the consequences of their actions.

683 · Be quick to take advantage of an advantage.

684 · Don't expect the best gifts to come wrapped in pretty paper.

685 · You may be fortunate and make a lot of money. But be sure your work involves something that enriches your spirit as well as your bank account.

686 · When a good man or woman runs for political office, support him or her with your time and money.

687 · When you need professional advice, get it from professionals, not from your friends.

688 · Remember that silence is sometimes the best answer.

689 · Don't buy a cheap mattress.

690 · Don't think you can relax your way to happiness. Happiness comes as a result of *doing*.

691 · Don't dismiss a good idea simply because you don't like the source.

692 · Send a poor child to summer camp.

693 · Choose a church that sings joyful music.

694 · What you must do, do cheerfully.

695 · Don't waste time waiting for inspiration. Begin, and inspiration will find you.

696 · Don't believe all you hear, spend all you have, or sleep all you want.

697 · When you say, "I love you," mean it.

698 · When you say, "I'm sorry," look the person in the eye.

699 · Conduct yourself in such a way that your high school would want you to address the graduating seniors.

700 · Be engaged at least six months before you get married.

701 · Win without boasting.

702 · Lose without excuses.

703 · Watch your attitude. It's the first thing people notice about you.

704 · Pack a light bathrobe on overnight trips. Take your pillow, too.

705 · Choose the apartment on the top floor.

706 • Ask someone you'd like to know better to list five people he would most like to meet. It will tell you a lot about him.

707 • Don't be a person who says, "Ready, fire, aim."

708 • Don't be a person who says, "Ready, aim, aim, aim."

709 • Deadlines are important. Meet them.

710 ◆ When you find someone doing small things well, put him or her in charge of bigger things.

711 ◆ Read more books.

712 ◆ Watch less TV.

713 ◆ Remember that a good price is not necessarily what an object is marked, but what it is worth to you.

714 · When opportunity knocks, invite it to stay for dinner.

715 · Remember that the more you know, the less you fear.

716 · When a waitress or waiter provides exceptional service, leave a generous tip, plus a short note like, "Thanks for the wonderful service. You made our meal a special experience."

717 · Remove your sunglasses when you talk to someone.

718 · Buy three best-selling children's books. Read them and then give them to a youngster.

719 · Introduce yourself to your neighbors as soon as you move into a new neighborhood.

720 · When a friend or loved one becomes ill, remember that hope and positive thinking are strong medicines.

721 · When you find something you really want, don't let a few dollars keep you from getting it.

722 · Be your children's best teacher and coach.

723 · Some things need doing better than they've ever been done before. Some just need doing. Others don't need doing at all. Know which is which.

724 · Buy ladders, extension cords, and garden hoses longer than you think you'll need.

725 · Don't confuse mere inconveniences with real problems.

726 · When asked to pray in public, be quick about it.

727 · Show extra respect for people whose jobs put dirt under their fingernails.

728 · Remember that a good example is the best sermon.

729 • Hold your child's hand every chance you get. The time will come all too soon when he or she won't let you.

730 • When you carve the Thanksgiving turkey, give the first piece to the person who prepared it.

731 • Live a good, honorable life. Then when you get older and think back, you'll get to enjoy it a second time.

732 · Wipe off the sticky honey jar before putting it back on the shelf.

733 · Purchase one piece of original art each year, even if it's just a small oil painting by a high school student.

734 · Volunteer to help a few hours a month working in a soup kitchen.

735 · Learn to juggle.

736 · Don't think people at the top of their professions have all the answers. They don't.

737 · Learn to make great spaghetti sauce. Your mother's recipe is the best.

738 · If you're treated unfairly by an airline, contact the Consumer Affairs Office of the Department of Transportation at (202) 366-2220.

739 · Get a car with a sun roof.

740 · Don't carry expensive luggage. It's a tip-off to thieves that expensive items may be inside.

741 · When traveling by plane, don't pack valuables or important papers in your suitcase. Carry them on board with you.

742 · Keep your private thoughts private.

743 ・ Put your jacket around your girlfriend on a chilly evening.

744 ・ Once every couple of months enjoy a four-course meal—only eat each course at a different restaurant.

745 ・ Introduce yourself to someone you would like to meet by smiling and saying, "My name is Adam Brown. I haven't had the pleasure of meeting you."

746 · Be humble and polite, but don't let anyone push you around.

747 · Put the strap around your neck before looking through binoculars.

748 · Do 100 push-ups every day: 50 in the morning and 50 in the evening.

749 · Wear goggles when operating a Weed Eater or power saw.

750 · Wrap a couple of thick rubber bands around your wallet when you're fishing or hiking. This will prevent it from slipping out of your pocket.

751 · Don't expect bankers to come to your aid in a crunch.

752 · Be advised that when negotiating, if you don't get it in writing, you probably won't get it.

753 ✦ Don't do business with anyone who has a history of suing people.

754 ✦ Every so often let your spirit of adventure triumph over your good sense.

755 ✦ Use a favorite picture of a loved one as a bookmark.

756 ✦ Never lose your nerve, your temper, or your car keys.

757 · Trust in God
but lock your car.

758 · Surprise an old friend with a phone call.

759 · Get involved at your child's school.

760 · Champion your wife. Be her best friend and biggest fan.

761 · Add to your children's private library by giving them a hardback copy of one of the classics every birthday. Begin with their first birthday.

762 · Carry a list of your wife's important sizes in your wallet.

763 · Don't open credit card bills on the weekend.

764 · Mind the store. No one cares about your business the way you do.

765 · Don't say no until you've heard the whole story.

766 · When you are a dinner guest, take a second helping if it's offered, but never a third.

767 · Never say anything uncomplimentary about your wife or children in the presence of others.

768 · Before going to bed on Christmas Eve, join hands with your family and sing "Silent Night."

769 • Don't accept unacceptable behavior.

770 • Never put the car in "drive" until all passengers have buckled up.

771 • When eating at a restaurant that features foreign food, don't order anything you can fix at home.

772 • Send your mother-in-law flowers on your wife's birthday.

773 · Write your pastor a note and tell him how much he means to you.

774 · Write your favorite author a note of appreciation.

775 · Apologize immediately when you lose your temper, especially to children.

776 · Buy your fiancée the nicest diamond engagement ring you can afford.

777 · When giving a speech, concentrate on what you can give the audience, not what you can get from them.

778 · Don't be so concerned with your rights that you forget your manners.

779 · When you're uncertain of what you should pay someone, ask, "What do you think is fair?" You'll almost always get a reasonable answer.

780 · Don't let weeds grow
around your dreams.

781 · When you know that someone has gone to a lot of trouble to get dressed up, tell them they look terrific!

782 · A loving atmosphere in your home is so important. Do all you can to create a tranquil, harmonious home.

783 · When you tell a child to do something, don't follow it with, "Okay?" Ask instead, "Do you understand?"

784 · Remember that almost everything looks better after a good night's sleep.

785 · Avoid using the word *impacted* unless you are describing wisdom teeth.

786 · Use a camcorder to videotape the contents of your home for insurance purposes. Don't forget closets and drawers. Keep the tape in your bank safe-deposit box.

787 · Read William Safire's collection of the world's great speeches, *Lend Me Your Ears* (W. W. Norton & Co., 1992).

788 · Keep a separate shaving kit packed for traveling.

789 · Remember that *how* you say something is as important as *what* you say.

790 · Every so often watch "Sesame Street."

791 · Read between the lines.

792 · Get to garage sales early. The good stuff is usually gone by 8:00 A.M.

793 · Stop and watch stonemasons at work.

794 · Stop and watch a farmer plowing a field.

795 · If your town has a baseball team, attend the season opener.

796 · When you see visitors taking pictures of each other, offer to take a picture of their group together.

797 · In disagreements with loved ones, deal with the current situation. Don't bring up the past.

798 · Never apologize for extreme measures when defending your values, your health, or your family's safety.

799 · Don't think you can fill an emptiness in your heart with money.

800 · Became famous for finishing important, difficult tasks.

801 · Never sell your teddy bear, letter sweater, or high school yearbooks at a garage sale. You'll regret it later.

802 · Leave a quarter where a child can find it.

803 · Don't take good
friends, good health,
or a good marriage
for granted.

804 · Place a note reading "Your license number has been reported to the police" on the windshield of a car illegally parked in a handicapped space.

805 · Buy a new tie to wear to your wedding rehearsal dinner. Wear it only once. Keep it forever.

806 · When you're lost, admit it, and ask for directions.

807 · Never buy just one roll of toilet paper, one roll of film, or one jar of peanut butter. Get two.

808 · Do a good job because you want to, not because you have to. This puts you in charge instead of your boss.

809 · Remember that the shortest way to get anywhere is to have good company traveling with you.

810 · Never type a love letter. Use a fountain pen.

811 · Never buy a chair or sofa without first sitting on it for several minutes.

812 · Don't be thin-skinned. Take criticism as well as praise with equal grace.

813 · At the end of your days, be leaning forward—not falling backwards.

814 • Never eat liver at a restaurant. Some things should be done only in the privacy of one's home.

815 • Keep impeccable tax records.

816 • Clean out a different drawer in your house every week.

817 • Share your knowledge. It's a way to achieve immortality.

818 · Be gentle
with the Earth.

819 · Don't work for a company led by someone of questionable character.

820 · When working with contractors, include a penalty clause in your contract for their not finishing on time.

821 · Read bulletin boards at the grocery store, college bookstore, and coin laundry. You will find all sorts of interesting things there.

822 · The next time you're standing next to a
police officer, firefighter, or paramedic,
tell them that you appreciate what they
do for the community.

823 · Learn three knock-knock jokes so you
will always be ready to entertain
children.

824 · Spend your time and energy creating,
not criticizing.

825 · Visit your old high school and introduce yourself to the principal. Ask if you can sit in on a couple of classes.

826 · Respect sailboats, snowmobiles, and motorcycles. They can teach you a painful lesson very fast.

827 · Act with courtesy and fairness regardless of how others treat you. Don't let them determine your response.

828 · In a verbal confrontation, lower your voice to the degree that the other person raises his or hers.

829 · Let your children see you do things for your wife that lets them know how much you love and treasure her.

830 · Take photographs of every car you own. Later, these photos will trigger wonderful memories.

831 · Don't allow children to ride in the back of a pickup truck.

832 · When you are a dinner guest at a restaurant, don't order anything more expensive than your host does.

833 · When someone offers to pay you now or later, choose now.

834 · Don't leave hair in the shower drain.

835 · When traveling the backroads, stop whenever you see a sign that reads "Honey For Sale."

836 · Start every day with the most important thing you have to do. Save the less important tasks for later.

837 · Think twice before deciding not to charge for your work. People often don't value what they don't pay for.

838 · Don't outlive your money.

839 · Never grab at a falling knife.

840 · Never take what you cannot use.

841 · When there is a hill to climb, don't think that waiting will make it smaller.

842 · When your dog dies, frame its collar and put it above a window facing west.

843 · When a garment label warns "Dry Clean Only," believe it.

844 · Don't eat any meat loaf but your mom's.

845 · Write the date and the names of non-family members on the backs of all photos as soon as you get them back from the developer.

846 · Help a child plant a small garden.

847 · Pray. There is
immeasurable power
in it.

848 · Don't take 11 items to the 10 Items Express Check-Out Lane.

849 · Don't call a fishing rod a "pole," a line a "rope," a rifle a "gun," or a ship a "boat."

850 · At meetings, resist turning around to see who has just arrived late.

851 · Don't ride a bicycle or motorcycle barefooted.

852 · Just because you earn a decent wage, don't look down on those who don't. To put things in perspective, consider what would happen to the public good if you didn't do your job for 30 days. Next, consider the consequences if sanitation workers didn't do their jobs for 30 days. Now, whose job is more important?

853 · Don't purchase anything in a package that appears to have been opened.

854 · Refuse to share personal and financial information unless you feel it is absolutely essential.

855 · Don't do business with people who knock on your door and say, "I just happened to be in the neighborhood."

856 · Choose a business partner the way you choose a tennis partner. Select someone who's strong where you are weak.

857 ◆ Call a nursing home or retirement center and ask for a list of the residents who seldom get mail or visitors. Send them a card several times a year. Sign it, "Someone who thinks you are very special."

858 ◆ Make duplicates of all important keys.

859 ◆ Read a lot when you're on vacation, but nothing that has to do with your business.

860 · Put the knife in the jelly *before* putting it in the peanut butter when you make a sandwich.

861 · Never buy a house in a neighborhood where you have to pay before pumping gas.

862 · Remember that what's right isn't always popular, and what's popular isn't always right.

863 · Before buying a house or renting an apartment, check the water pressure by turning on the faucets and the shower and then flushing the toilet.

864 · Overestimate travel time by 15 percent.

865 · Properly fitting shoes should feel good as soon as you try them on. Don't believe the salesperson who says, "They'll be fine as soon as you break them in."

866 · Schedule your bachelor party at least two days before your wedding.

867 · Get a haircut a week before the big interview.

868 · Spend your life lifting people up, not putting people down.

869 · Never interrupt when you are being flattered.

870 · Remember that great love and great achievements involve great risk.

871 · Don't pick up after your children. That's their job.

872 · Own a cowboy hat.

873 · Own a comfortable chair for reading.

874 · Own a set of good kitchen knives.

875 · In business or in life, don't follow the wagon tracks too closely.

876 · Get your name off mailing lists by writing to: Mail Preference Service, 11 W. 42nd St., P.O. Box 3861, New York, NY 10163-3861.

877 · Brush your teeth before putting on your tie.

878 · Never risk what you can't afford to lose.

879 · Mind your own business.

880 · Don't trust a woman who doesn't close her eyes when you kiss her.

881 · Never tell a man he's losing his hair. He already knows.

882 · Learn to use a needle and thread, a steam iron, and an espresso machine.

883 · Remember that the "suggested retail price" seldom is.

884 · Never say, "My child would never do that."

885 · Once a year, go someplace you've never been before.

886 · Replace the batteries in smoke alarms every January 1st.

887 · Never order chicken-fried steak in a place that doesn't have a jukebox.

888 · Remember that ignorance is expensive.

889 · Keep candles and matches in the kitchen and bedroom in case of power failure.

890 · If you make a lot of money, put it to use helping others while you are living. That is wealth's greatest satisfaction.

891 · Listen to your critics. They will keep you focused and innovative.

892 · Never tell a person who's experiencing deep sorrow, "I know how you feel." You don't.

893 · Remember that not getting what you want is sometimes a stroke of good luck.

894 · Never say anything to a news reporter that you don't want to see on the front page of your local paper. Comments made "off the record" seldom are.

895 · Remember the old proverb, "Out of debt, out of danger."

896 · Don't allow your dog to bark and disturb the neighbors.

897 · When declaring your rights, don't forget your responsibilities.

898 · Remember that what you give will afford you more pleasure than what you get.

899 · Display your street number prominently on your mailbox or house in case emergency vehicles need to find you.

900 · Think twice before accepting a job that requires you to work in an office with no windows.

901 · Remember that everyone you meet wears an invisible sign. It reads, "Notice me. Make me feel important."

902 · Never hire someone you wouldn't invite home to dinner.

903 · Perform your job better than anyone else can. That's the best job security I know.

904 · When camping or hiking, never leave evidence that you were there.

905 · Dress respectfully when attending church.

906 · Never ask an accountant, lawyer, or doctor professional questions in a social setting.

907 · When someone has provided you with exceptional service, write a note to his or her boss.

908 · If you've learned that a good friend is ill, don't ask him about it. Let him tell you first.

909 · For easier reading in motel rooms, pack your own 100-watt light bulb.

910 · If you lend someone money, make sure his character exceeds the collateral.

911 · Whether it's life or a horse that throws you, get right back on.

912 · Be cautious telling people how contented and happy you are. Many will resent it.

913 · Hang up if someone puts you on hold to take a "call waiting."

914 · Accept the fact that regardless of how many times you are right, you will sometimes be wrong.

915 · Every once in a while ask yourself the question, If money weren't a consideration, what would I like to be doing?

916 · Learn the rules.
Then break some.

917 • No matter how old you get, hug and kiss your mother whenever you greet her.

918 • Watch "The Andy Griffith Show" to help put things in perspective.

919 • Put love notes in your child's lunch box.

920 • Encourage anyone who is trying to improve mentally, physically, or spiritually.

921 · Remember that half the joy of achievement is in the anticipation.

922 · Go to rodeos.

923 · Go to donkey basketball games.

924 · Go to chili cook-offs.

925 · Order an L. L. Bean catalog. Write L. L. Bean, Freeport, ME 04033.

926 · Remember that the best relationship is one where your love for each other is greater than your need for each other.

927 · When you need assistance, ask this way: "I've got a problem. I wonder if you would be kind enough to help me?"

928 · Get involved with your local government. As someone said, "Politics is too important to be left to the politicians."

929 • Order a Sundance catalog. Write: Customer Service Center, 1909 South 4250 West, Salt Lake City, UT 84104.

930 • Never swap your integrity for money, power, or fame.

931 • Never tell an off-color joke when ladies are present.

932 • Never sell yourself short.

933 • Fool someone on April 1st.

934 • Never remind someone of a kindness or act of generosity you have shown him or her. Bestow a favor and then forget it.

935 • Help your children set up their own savings and checking accounts by age 16.

936 • Learn to play "Amazing Grace" on the piano.

937 · Put on old clothes before you get out the paint brushes.

938 · Never be ashamed of your patriotism.

939 · Never be ashamed of honest tears.

940 · Never be ashamed of laughter that's too loud or singing that's too joyful.

941 · Always try the house dressing.

942 · Don't trust your memory; write it down.

943 · When you get really angry, stick your hands in your pockets.

944 · Do all you can to increase the salaries of good teachers.

945 · At least once, date a woman with beautiful red hair.

946 · Visit friends and relatives when they are in the hospital. You only need to stay a few minutes.

947 · Watch the movie *Mr. Smith Goes to Washington*.

948 · Watch the movie *Regarding Henry*.

949 · Never leave a youngster in the car without taking the car keys.

950 · Don't think that sending a gift or flowers substitutes for your presence.

951 · When visiting a small town at lunch time, choose the café on the square.

952 · Attach a small Christmas wreath to your car's grill on the first day of December.

953 · Never ask a barber if you need a haircut.

954 · Truth is serious business. When criticizing others, remember that a little goes a long way.

955 · Never buy a piece of jewelry that costs more than $100 without doing a little haggling.

956 · When your children are learning to play musical instruments, buy them good ones.

957 · Judge your success by what you had to give up in order to get it.

958 • Never "borrow" so much as a pencil from your workplace.

959 • Become a tourist for a day in your own hometown. Take a tour. See the sights.

960 • Don't confuse foolishness with bravery.

961 • Don't mistake kindness for weakness.

962 • Answer the easy questions first.

963 • Don't discuss domestic problems at work.

964 • A racehorse that consistently runs just a second faster than another horse is worth millions of dollars more. Be willing to give that extra effort that separates the winner from the one in second place.

965 • Create a smoke-free office and home.

966 • Let some things remain mysterious.

967 · Never ignore evil.

968 · Be especially courteous and patient with older people.

969 · Remember this statement by Coach Lou Holtz, "Life is 10 percent what happens to me and 90 percent how I react to it."

970 · Travel. See new places, but remember to take along an open mind.

971 · Never get a tattoo.

972 · Never eat a sugared doughnut when wearing a dark suit.

973 · Call before dropping in on friends and family.

974 · When you are away from home and hear church bells, think of someone who loves you.

975 · When friends offer to help, let them.

976 · Never decide to do nothing just because you can only do a little. Do what you can.

977 · Acknowledge a gift, no matter how small.

978 · Every now and then, bite off more than you can chew.

979 · Remember that your character is your destiny.

980 · Aproach love and cooking with reckless abandon.

981 · Grind it out. Hanging on just one second longer than your competition makes you the winner.

982 · Buy and use your customers' products.

983 · Be better prepared than you think you will need to be.

984 · Buy a small, inexpensive camera. Take it with you everywhere.

985 · Let your handshake be as binding as a signed contract.

986 · Keep and file the best business letters you receive.

987 · Pay the extra $10 for the best seats at a play or concert.

988 · Give handout materials after your presentation, never before.

989 • Never buy anything from a rude salesperson, no matter how much you want it.

990 • Get a flu shot.

991 • Worry makes for a hard pillow. When something's troubling you, before going to sleep, jot down three things you can do the next day to help solve the problem.

992 · Buy a red umbrella. It's easier to find among all the black ones, and it adds a little color to rainy days.

993 · Hire people more for their judgment than for their talents.

994 · Love someone who doesn't deserve it.

995 · Every so often, go where you can hear a wooden screen door slam shut.

996 • When you mean no, say it in a way that's not ambiguous.

997 • Attend a high school football game. Sit near the band.

998 • Give children toys that are powered by their imagination, not by batteries.

999 • Remember that your child's character is like good soup. Both are homemade.

1000 · Never open a restaurant.

1001 · When you're buying something that you only need to buy once, buy the best you can afford.

1002 · As soon as you get married, start saving for your children's education.

1003 · Reject and condemn prejudice based on race, gender, religion, or age.

1004 • Choose a seat in the row next to the emergency exit when flying. You will get more leg room.

1005 • Get involved with Habitat for Humanity and help build housing for the poor. Call 1-800-HABITAT.

1006 • You may dress unconventionally, but remember that the more strangely you dress, the better you have to be.

1007 · Life is short.
Eat more pancakes
and fewer rice cakes.

1008 · Be suspicious of a boss who schedules
meetings instead of making decisions.

1009 · Carry three business cards in your wallet.

1010 · Regardless of the situation, react with
class.

1011 · For emergencies, always have a quarter in
your pocket and a ten dollar bill hidden
in your wallet.

1012 · Don't overfeed horses or brothers-in-law.

1013 · Be able to hit consistently four out of five at the free-throw line.

1014 · Become the kind of person who brightens a room just by entering it.

1015 · Remember the observation of William James that the deepest principle in human nature is the craving to be appreciated.

1016 · Buy raffle tickets, candy bars, and baked goods from students who are raising money for school projects.

1017 · Be wary of the man who's "all hat and no cattle."

1018 · Borrow a box of puppies for an afternoon and take them to visit the residents of a retirement home. Stand back and watch the smiles.

1019 · Reread Thoreau's *Walden*.

1020 · When there's a piano to be moved, don't reach for the stool.

1021 · Someone will always be looking at you as an example of how to behave. Don't let them down.

1022 · Go on blind dates. Remember, that's how I met your mother.

1023 • Root for the home team.

1024 • Follow your own star.

1025 • Remember the ones who love you.

1026 • Go home for the holidays.

1027 • Don't get too big for your britches.

1028 • Call your dad.

Dear Reader,

If you received advice from your parents or grand-parents that was especially meaningful and you would like me to share it with other readers, please write and tell me about it.

I look forward to hearing from you.

H. Jackson Brown, Jr.
P. O. Box 150155
Nashville, Tn 37215